THE WORLD OF PLANTS

HOW DO MEAT-EATING PLANTS CATCH THEIR FOOD?

by Ruth Owen

PowerKiDS press.

New York

Published in 2015 by The Rosen Publishing Group, Inc.
29 East 21st Street, New York, NY 10010

First Edition

Produced for Rosen by Ruby Tuesday Books Ltd
Editor for Ruby Tuesday Books Ltd: Mark J. Sachner
US Editor: Joshua Shadowens
Designer: Emma Randall

Photo Credits:
Cover, 1, 4–5, 6–7, 8–9, 10–11, 12–13, 15, 16, 18, 22–23, 24–25, 26, 27 (bottom), 29 © Shutterstock; 14 © Barbara Page; 17, 20 © FLPA; 19 © Noah Elhardt; 21 © Chien Lee; 27 (top) © Petr Dlouhy.

Publisher's Cataloging Data

Owen, Ruth.
How do meat-eating plants catch their food? / by Ruth Owen, first edition.
p. cm. — (The world of plants)
Includes index.
ISBN 978-1-4777-7153-2 (library binding) — ISBN 978-1-4777-7154-9 (pbk.) —
ISBN 978-1-4777-7155-6 (6-pack)
1. Carnivorous plants — Juvenile literature. I. Owen, Ruth, 1967–. II. Title.
QK926.O94 2015
580—d23

Manufactured in the United States of America

CPSIA Compliance Information: Batch #WS14PK8: For Further Information contact Rosen Publishing, New York, New York at 1-800-237-9932

Contents

Meat Eaters

Many meat eaters hunt their **prey**. They stalk and pounce. They chase and attack with sharp claws and savage teeth. There are some meat eaters, however, that cannot use these tactics.

Some meat eaters cannot run or jump. They have no claws or teeth. These **carnivorous** living things must use a different set of tactics to catch their food. These meat eaters use traps, tricks, and even glue to capture their prey. Once caught, however, the victim's end is the same. All the struggling creature can do is give in and wait to become the meal of a carnivorous plant.

Around the world there are many different **species** of meat-eating plants. But why do some plants capture animals as food? And how do they do it?

A Venus flytrap

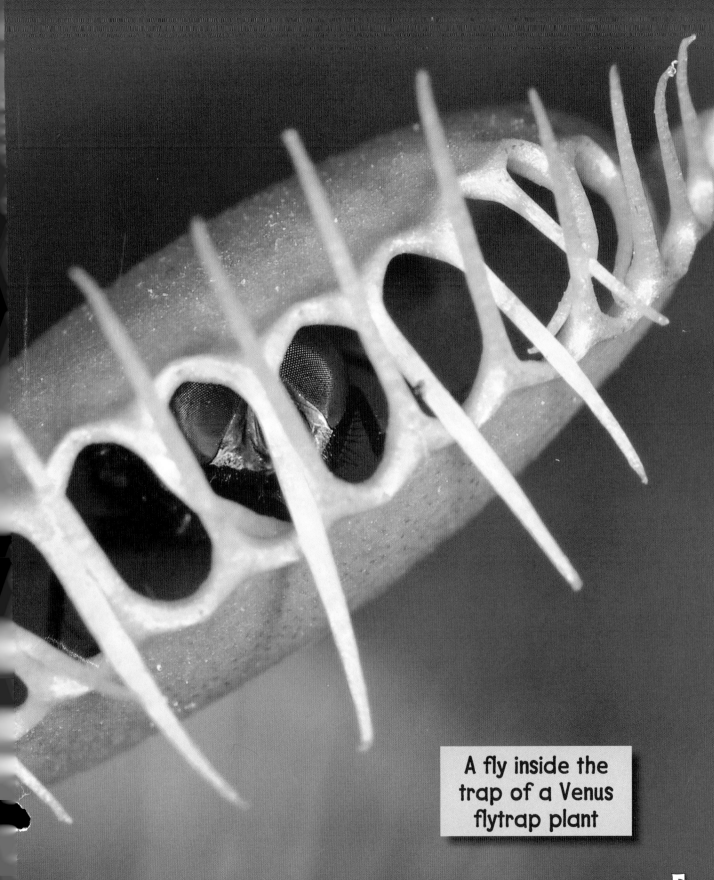

A fly inside the trap of a Venus flytrap plant

Food For Energy

In order to grow and survive, carnivorous plants need food for energy. They also need additional **nutrients** to help them remain healthy.

All plants, including meat-eaters, make the food they need for energy from water, **carbon dioxide**, and sunlight. This process is called **photosynthesis**, and it takes place in the plant's leaves.

Plants big and small use sunlight, carbon dioxide, and water to make food.

A plant takes in water from the soil with its **roots**. The water is then delivered through the plant's stems to its leaves. The leaves take in carbon dioxide from the air through **microscopic** holes called **stomata**. Then, inside the plant's leaves, a substance called **chlorophyll** traps the energy in sunlight and uses it to turn the water and carbon dioxide into a sugary food. All plants use this type of food for energy.

Carnivorous plants make the food they need for energy through photosynthesis.

7

Nutrients for Growth and Health

A plant cannot get everything it needs for growth and health during photosynthesis. Plants also need to take in nutrients.

Nutrients are essential to help plants grow and produce leaves, flowers, and seeds. Nutrients such as nitrogen, potassium, calcium, and magnesium can be found dissolved in water in the soil. Most plants take in these nutrients through their roots when they take in water.

These garden plants are growing in soil containing plenty of nutrients.

A Venus flytrap growing in a rocky habitat

Some plants, however, live in **habitats**, such as **bogs** or rocky places, where there is not much soil, or the soil contains few nutrients. These plants have developed an alternative way to obtain the nutrients they need. They get them from the bodies of animals!

Carnivorous pitcher plants growing in a boggy habitat

Venus Flytraps

Venus flytraps are carnivorous plants that grow in boggy habitats. These plants are only found growing wild in a few small areas on the East Coast of the United States.

Some of the leaves of a Venus flytrap plant act as deadly traps for catching prey. To attract their prey, the traps produce a sweet liquid called **nectar**. Flies and other insects land on the traps to feed on the nectar. Inside the traps there are tiny trigger hairs. When an insect touches these hairs, the trap is triggered and snaps shut! The more the plant's victim struggles, the tighter the trap closes.

The traps on a Venus flytrap are edged with tooth-like projections called cilia. These projections lace together to ensure that the trap stays tightly shut.

Trap

Trigger hairs

Insect

Cilia

Venus flytrap

Dinner Time for a Venus Flytrap

Once an insect is trapped by a Venus flytrap, there is no escape for the little creature.

The cilia on this trap are holding it tightly closed.

This trap has been opened to show the partly digested insect inside.

Now the trap's role changes. In fact, it becomes a lot like a tiny stomach. Juices begin to ooze from the trap. These juices act like the digestive juices that break down food in your stomach. Over several days, the juices from the trap dissolve the soft parts of the insect, turning them into a soft, soupy mass. Then the trap absorbs nutrients, such as nitrogen, from this mass.

After about 12 days, all that remains of the insect is its hard **exoskeleton**. The trap reopens and the dried-up husk of the insect is blown away by the wind, or washed from the trap next time it rains.

Plants That Drown Their Victims

Some carnivorous plants lure their prey with the promise of a sweet meal of nectar. Then they drown them!

There are many different species of meat-eating **pitcher** plants. They come in lots of shapes and sizes, but all have a cup or tube-like part called a pitcher. Inside the pitcher is a deadly pool of watery liquid where the plants' victims drown.

Pitcher plants growing in a bog

Cup-like pitchers dangle from the plant on a thin tendril.

The liquid inside a pitcher contains juices that dissolve any soft, fleshy parts of an animal, releasing nutrients into the liquid. Then the pitcher absorbs the nutrients from the liquid. Finally, all that remains of the pitcher plant's victim is its dry empty exoskeleton!

Tendril

Pitcher

North American Pitcher Plants

North American pitcher plants grow in bogs and other places where the ground is very wet.

These meat-eaters attract insects to the rims of their tube-like pitchers with nectar. The rims of the pitchers are dangerously slippery, however. When an insect lands on a pitcher's rim it starts to feed, but may soon lose its footing. Then it will plunge into the liquid at the base of the pitcher.

If the wet, panicked creature tries to climb out of the pitcher, it finds there is no escape. The inside walls of the pitcher are very slippery and contain downward-pointing hairs that make climbing upward nearly impossible. All the plant's victim can do is wait to be digested!

North American pitcher plants

Rim

Ant feeding on nectar

Downward-pointing hairs

Liquid in pitcher

Drowned ant

Trapping with Tricks

California pitcher plants have a range of horrible tricks to trap and kill their victims.

Insects enter the plant's bubble-like hoods to feed on nectar. The inside surface of the hood is slippery, though, so an insect may slip and fall down into the pitcher. If an insect avoids slipping, it soon finds that escaping from the hood is not so easy.

The many see-through patches in the hood look like exit holes, but they are not. The insect crawls from patch to patch looking for a way out. Finally, exhausted and trapped, it falls into the pitcher and drowns. California pitcher plants are nicknamed cobra lilies because they are shaped like a rearing cobra—complete with a leafy forked tongue.

Cobra

California pitcher plant

See-through patches

Bubble-like hood

Leaves

19

Giant Pitcher Plants

The cup-like pitchers of some pitcher plant species growing in tropical forests can grow to be very large.

One of the largest species ever discovered was found on a mountainside in the Philippines. A British explorer and scientist, Stewart McPherson, discovered the plant in 2007. The largest of the plant's pitchers were 11 inches (28 cm) long and could hold just over 3 pints (1.5 l) of liquid. Stewart called the new species *Nepenthes attenboroughii,* naming it after a famous British **naturalist**, Sir David Attenborough.

Like other pitcher plants, the main prey of giant pitchers is insects. Sometimes, however, larger animals such as rats, shrews, and lizards may fall into the pitchers. Unable to escape from the slippery cups, these creatures then die and become food for the plants.

A pitcher of *Nepenthes attenboroughii*

A rat feeding on nectar from a giant pitcher plant species

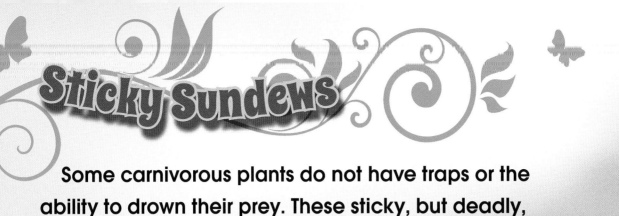

Sticky Sundews

Some carnivorous plants do not have traps or the ability to drown their prey. These sticky, but deadly, meat-eaters use glue-like substances to trap their food.

Sundews are carnivorous plants that grow in wet, boggy places almost everywhere around the world, except for the Arctic and Antarctica. There are about 160 different species of these plants.

Sundews are often just a few inches (cm) tall, so a person would need to look closely to see their amazing methods of trapping prey. The leaves of sundews are covered with tiny stalk-like **glands** that produce a sticky glue. Each stalk has a glistening blob of glue on its end that smells like nectar. As an insect flies by the plant it sees and smells the fake nectar and zooms in.

Blob of glue-like substance

Sundew leaves

Stalk

A sundew plant

No Escape

When an insect lands on a sundew leaf expecting a meal of nectar, it gets stuck!

One leg gets stuck, then another. The insect might beat its wings to aid its escape, only to find that they touch the blobs of glue and become stuck, too. As the insect struggles to escape, the leaf curls around its prey. Then, with the insect still fighting for its life, the leaf releases juices that start to dissolve the creature.

As the insect's body breaks down, the leaf absorbs nutrients from its meal. Once the leaf has absorbed all the nutrients it can, it uncurls, leaving just the dried-up shell of its victim.

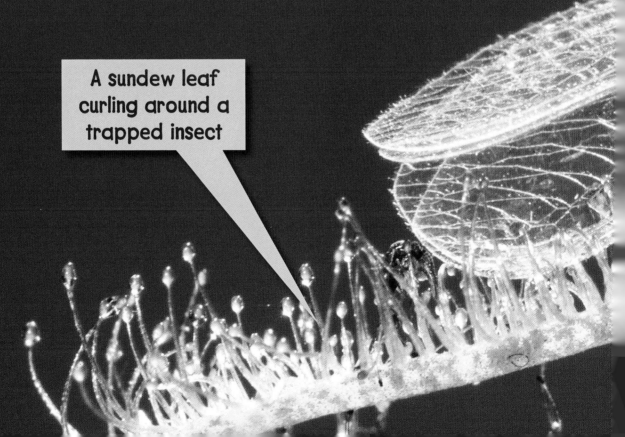

A sundew leaf curling around a trapped insect

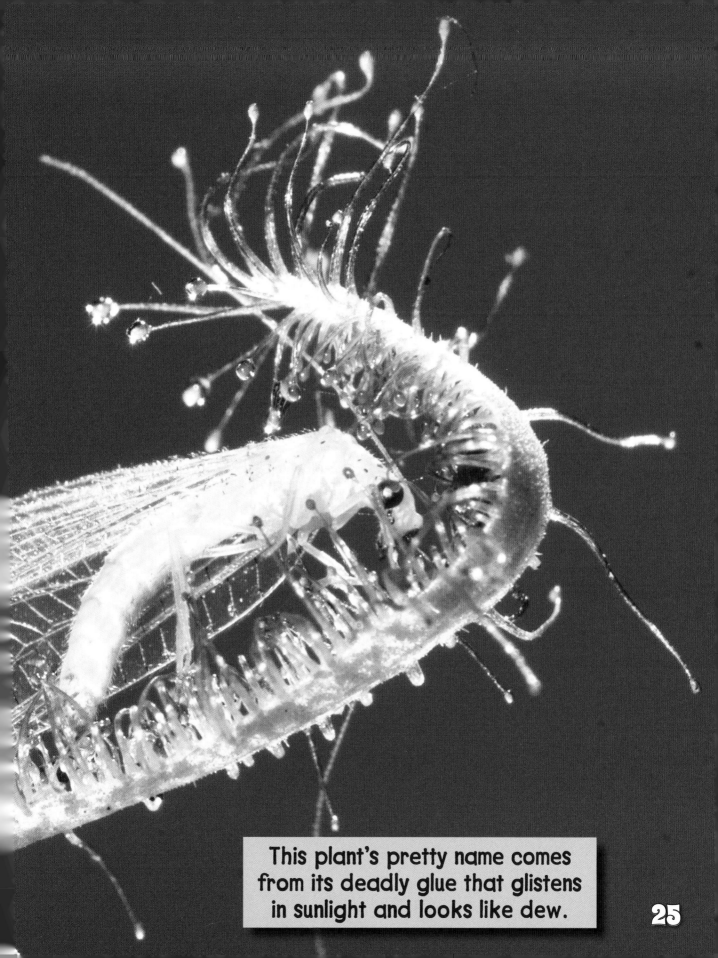

This plant's pretty name comes from its deadly glue that glistens in sunlight and looks like dew.

Pretty Dangerous

Like sundews, butterworts are small, pretty plants that hide a deadly secret.

A butterwort's leaves look as if they are covered with tiny drops of water or nectar. In fact, the pretty shine on the plant's leaves is glue that's produced by tiny hairs. Once an insect gets trapped in the glue, the leaf produces juices that turn the insect into a soupy mass so its nutrients can be absorbed by the leaf.

It's hard to imagine that plants can actually be hunters, but it's true. If you're an insect, these living things are as deadly as a lion or a shark. Carnivorous plants may have leaves instead of claws and teeth, but with their traps, tricks, and glue, these little meat-eaters are deadly killers!

A butterwort plant

This close-up view of a butterwort leaf shows the tiny hairs that produce glue for trapping prey.

Butterwort leaves

Investigating the World of Plants

Triggering the Trap

In order for a Venus flytrap trap to catch a meal, the plant's traps must close at exactly the right moment. Too soon and its prey may not be fully inside the trap and will be alerted to the danger. Too late and its prey will escape.

You will need:
- A Venus flytrap plant
- A magnifying glass
- A pencil
- A watch (for timing seconds)
- A notebook and pen

If the plant closes its trap on an object that is not an insect, it will waste valuable energy. Also, each trap can only snap shut three or four times before it loses its effectiveness. So each trap is precious and the plant can't afford to wear out its traps capturing objects, such as a piece of dead leaf, that land on the trap by accident.

A Venus flytrap's timing has to be just right, so let's investigate how it works in this activity.

You can buy Venus flytraps from many garden centers or homewares stores that sell plants. You can also order them online. If you are lucky enough to see these plants growing wild where you live, DO NOT remove them from their natural habitat.

Step 1:

Begin by taking a close-up look at the plant's traps through the magnifying glass.

Do you see the hairs inside the traps?

Does each trap have the same number of hairs?

Draw the following table in your notebook.

ACTION	TRAP 1 DID THE TRAP CLOSE?	TRAP 2 DID THE TRAP CLOSE?
Touch the cilia		
Touch one hair (inside the trap) one time		
Touch one hair two times (within 1 second)		
Touch one hair two times (with a 5 second interval)		
Touch one hair two times (with a 10 second interval)		
Touch one hair two times (with a 30 second interval)		

Step 3:

Now investigate how the traps operate by testing one of the traps carrying out the actions described in the table. Use the point of a pencil to gently touch the trap. Record your results in the table.

Step 4:

Now try again using a different trap, and record your results.

Why? How? What?

When did the traps shut? Why do you think the traps shut when they did and not at the other times? (See page 32 for the answer.)

Glossary

bogs (BOGZ) Natural habitats where the ground is soft and very wet, and lots of moss may grow. Bogs are usually part of a wetland.

carbon dioxide (KAHR-bun dy-OK-syd) A clear gas in the air that plants use to make food. When humans and other animals breathe out, they release carbon dioxide into the air.

carnivorous (kahr-NIH-vuh-rus) Referring to an animal or plant that eats, or obtains nutrients from, meat.

chlorophyll (KLOR-uh-fil) The substance that gives plants their green color. Leaves use chlorophyll for making food during photosynthesis.

exoskeleton (ek-soh-SKEH-leh-tun) The skeleton of animals such as insects and spiders that is on the outside of the body.

glands (GLANDZ) Organs that produce chemical substances in a plant or in an animal's body.

habitats (HA-buh-tats) Places where animals or plants normally live. A habitat may be a backyard, a forest, the ocean, or a mountainside.

microscopic (my-kreh-SKAH-pik) So small that an object can only be seen through a microscope and not with just a person's eyes alone.

naturalist (NA-chuh-ruh-list) An expert in natural history, often a scientist, who studies plants, animals, and natural habitats.

nectar (NEK-tur) A sweet liquid, produced by flowers, that many insects and other animals eat.

nutrients (NOO-tree-ents) Substances needed by a plant or animal to help it live and grow. Most plants take in nutrients from the soil using their roots. Carnivorous plants obtain nutrients from the bodies of animals.

photosynthesis (foh-toh-SIN-thuh-sus) The process by which plants make food in their leaves using water, carbon dioxide, and sunlight.

pitcher (PIH-cher) A tube or cup-shaped part of a carnivorous plant that contains a liquid that drowns and then dissolves the plant's prey.

prey (PRAY) An animal that is hunted by other animals for food.

roots (ROOTS) Parts of plants that usually grow underground and are used by the plant for taking in water and nutrients from the soil. Roots also hold a plant steady in soil so it doesn't fall over.

species (SPEE-sheez) One type of living thing. The members of a species look alike and can reproduce together.

stomata (STOH-mah-tuh) Microscopic holes on a leaf that a plant uses for taking in carbon dioxide and releasing oxygen.

Read More

Blashfield, Jean F. *Plant Life*. New York: Gareth Stevens, 2008.

Gould, Margee. *Meat-Eating Plants*. New York: PowerKids Press, 2012.

Preszler, June. *Meat-Eating Plants and Other Extreme Plant Life*. Mankato, MN: Capstone Press, 2008.

Index

Answers

TRIGGERING THE TRAP

The traps on your plant probably shut when you touched a hair inside them twice with an interval of around five to ten seconds. Just one touch on a hair did not trigger a trap because it might be an object, such as a piece of debris, falling into the trap by accident. Two touches close together, however, recreated the movement of an insect walking around inside the trap, so the trap closed.